GRAPHIC LIBRARY™

INVENTIONS AND DISCOVERY

GEORGE EASTMAN AND THE KODAK CAMERA

by Jennifer Fandel

illustrated by Gordon Purcell and Al Milgrom

Consultant:
David Silver, President
International Photographic
Historical Organization
San Francisco, California

Capstone *press*

Mankato, Minnesota

Graphic Library is published by Capstone Press,
151 Good Counsel Drive, P.O. Box 669, Mankato, Minnesota 56002.
www.capstonepress.com

Printed in the United States of America

1 2 3 4 5 6 12 11 10 09 08 07

Library of Congress Cataloging-in-Publication Data
Fandel, Jennifer.
George Eastman and the Kodak camera / by Jennifer Fandel; illustrated by Gordon Purcell and Al Milgrom
p. cm.—(Graphic library. Inventions and discovery)
Includes bibliographical references and index.
ISBN-13: 978-0-7368-6848-8 (hardcover)
ISBN-10: 0-7368-6848-8 (hardcover)
ISBN-13: 978-0-7368-7900-2 (softcover pbk.)
ISBN-10: 0-7368-7900-5 (softcover pbk)
1. Eastman, George, 1854-1932—Juvenile literature. 2. Photographic industry—United States—Biography—Juvenile literature. 3. Kodak camera—Juvenile literature. I. Purcell, Gordon, ill. II. Milgrom, Al, ill. III. Title. IV. Series.
TR140.E3F36 2007
770.92—dc22 [B] 2006036327

Summary: In graphic novel format, tells the story of how George Eastman developed the Kodak camera, and how his company changed the way people captured the moments of their lives.

Designer
Jason Knudson

Editor
Mandy Robbins

Colorist
Brent Schoonover

TABLE OF CONTENTS

CHAPTER 1
A HOBBY THAT CLICKED

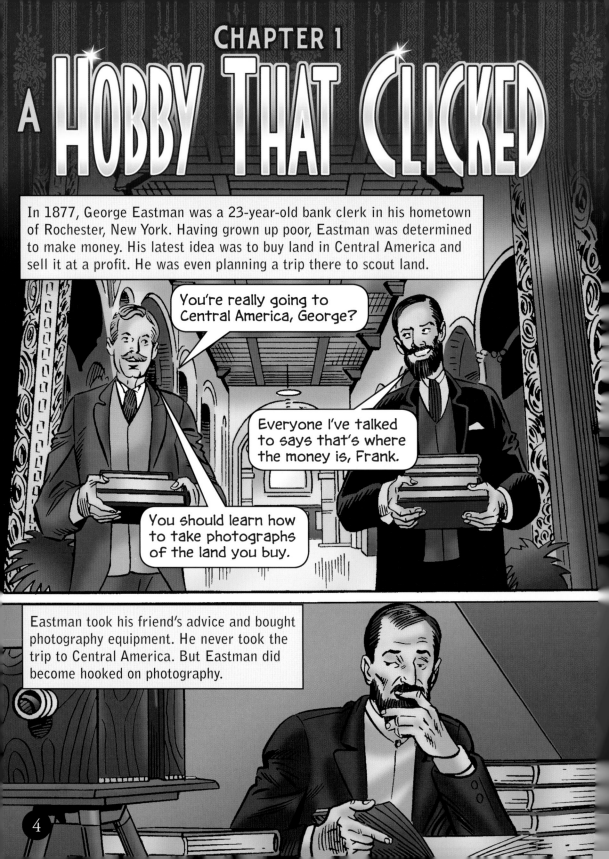

In 1877, George Eastman was a 23-year-old bank clerk in his hometown of Rochester, New York. Having grown up poor, Eastman was determined to make money. His latest idea was to buy land in Central America and sell it at a profit. He was even planning a trip there to scout land.

You're really going to Central America, George?

Everyone I've talked to says that's where the money is, Frank.

You should learn how to take photographs of the land you buy.

Eastman took his friend's advice and bought photography equipment. He never took the trip to Central America. But Eastman did become hooked on photography.

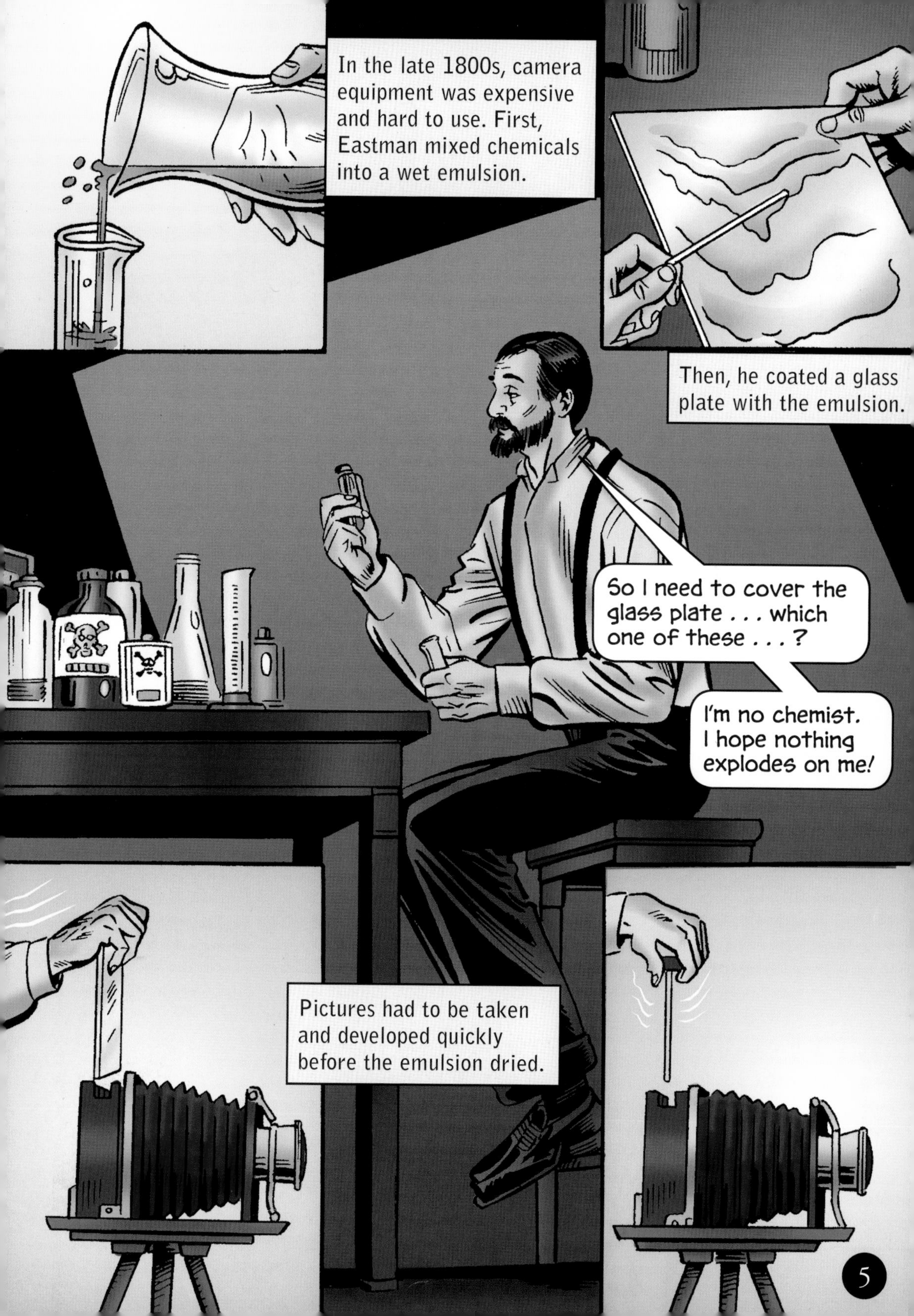

In the late 1800s, camera equipment was expensive and hard to use. First, Eastman mixed chemicals into a wet emulsion.
Then, he coated a glass plate with the emulsion.
So I need to cover the glass plate . . . which one of these . . . ?
I'm no chemist. I hope nothing explodes on me!
Pictures had to be taken and developed quickly before the emulsion dried.

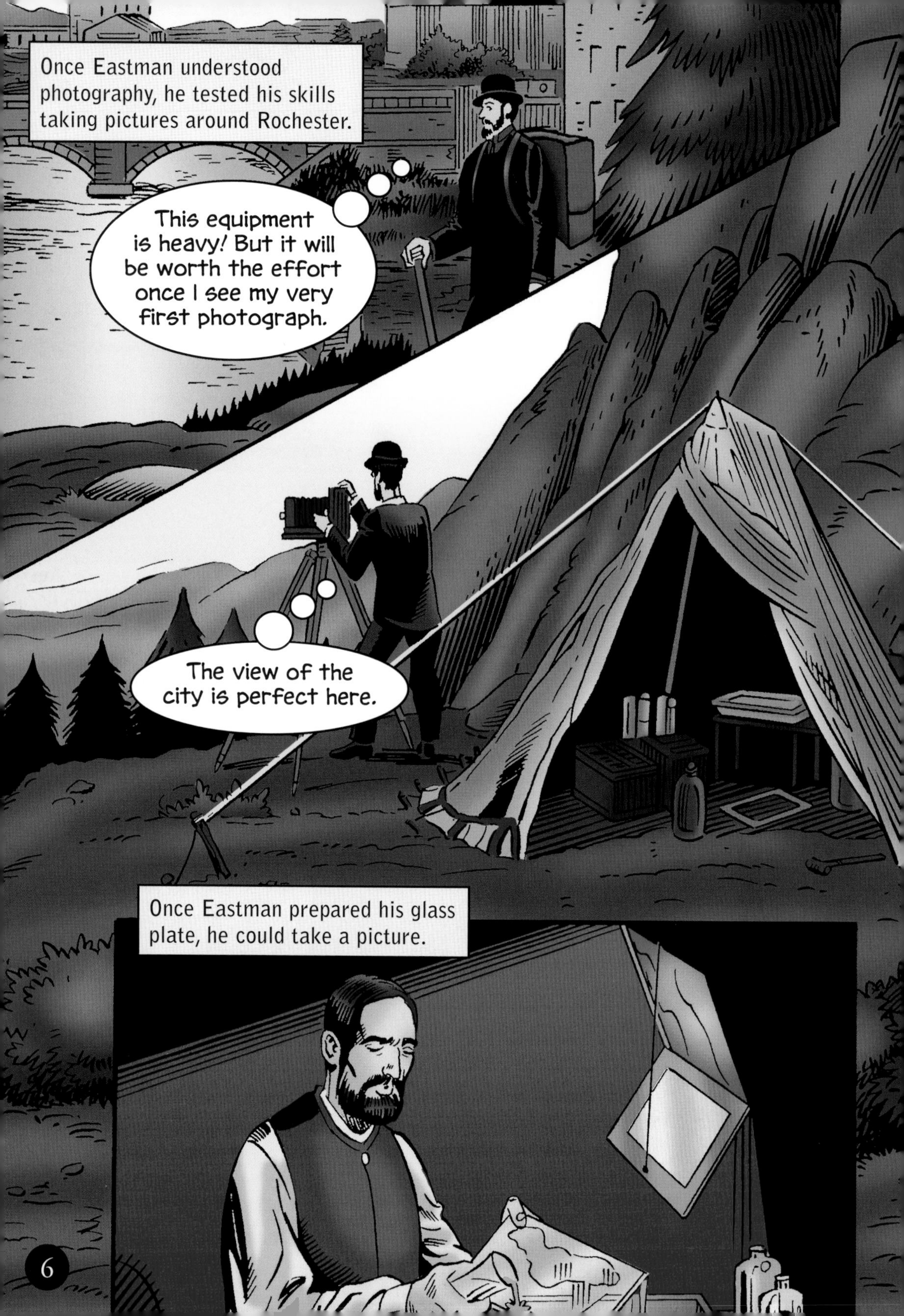
Once Eastman understood photography, he tested his skills taking pictures around Rochester.
This equipment is heavy! But it will be worth the effort once I see my very first photograph.
The view of the city is perfect here.
Once Eastman prepared his glass plate, he could take a picture.

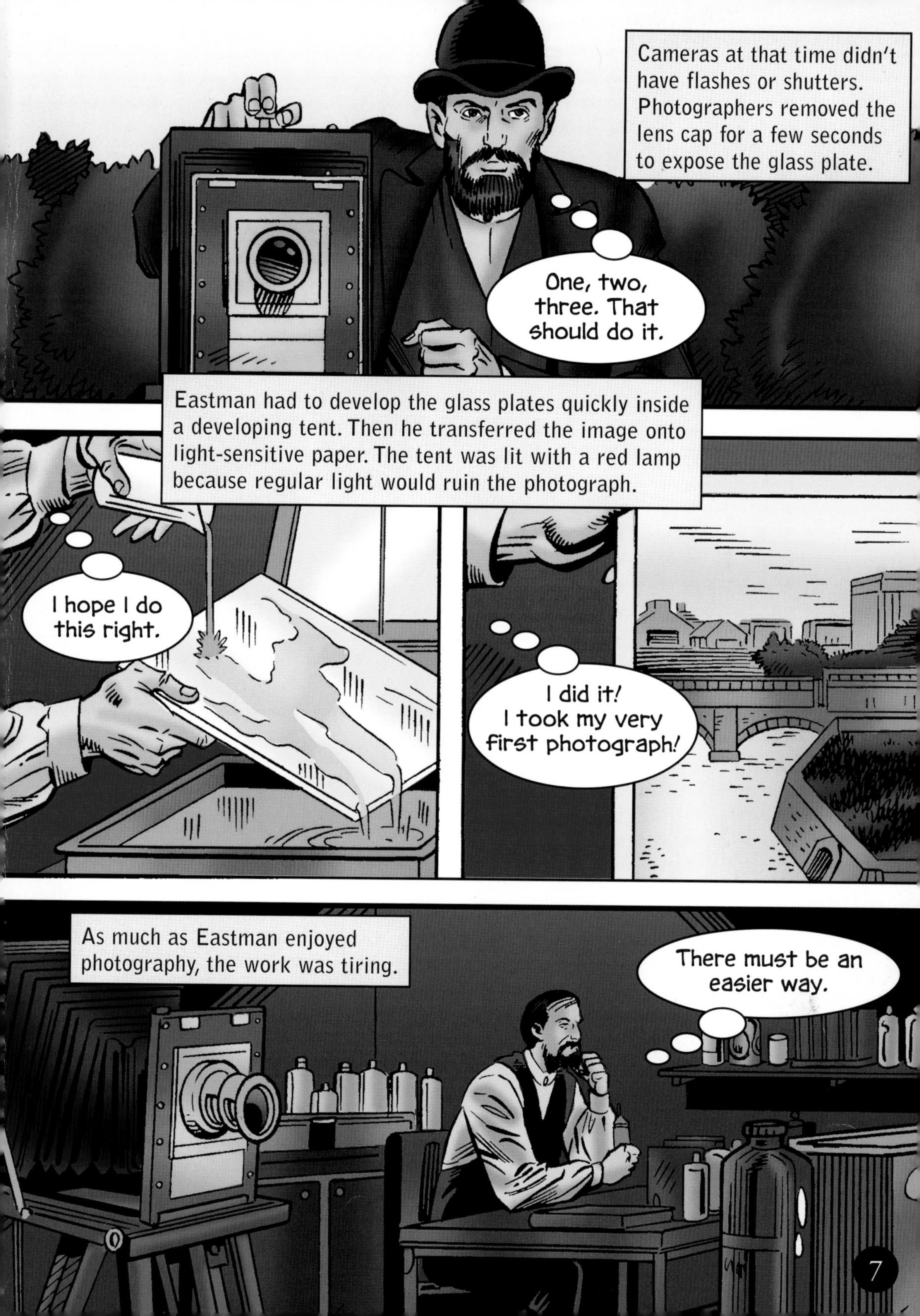
Cameras at that time didn't have flashes or shutters. Photographers removed the lens cap for a few seconds to expose the glass plate.
One, two, three. That should do it.
Eastman had to develop the glass plates quickly inside a developing tent. Then he transferred the image onto light-sensitive paper. The tent was lit with a red lamp because regular light would ruin the photograph.
I hope I do this right.
I did it! I took my very first photograph!
As much as Eastman enjoyed photography, the work was tiring.
There must be an easier way.

CHAPTER 2

A CLEAR AND SIMPLE DREAM

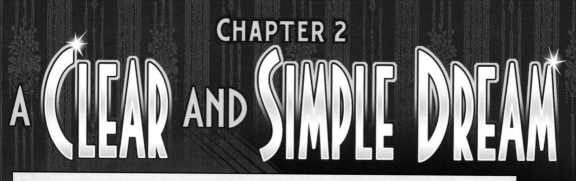

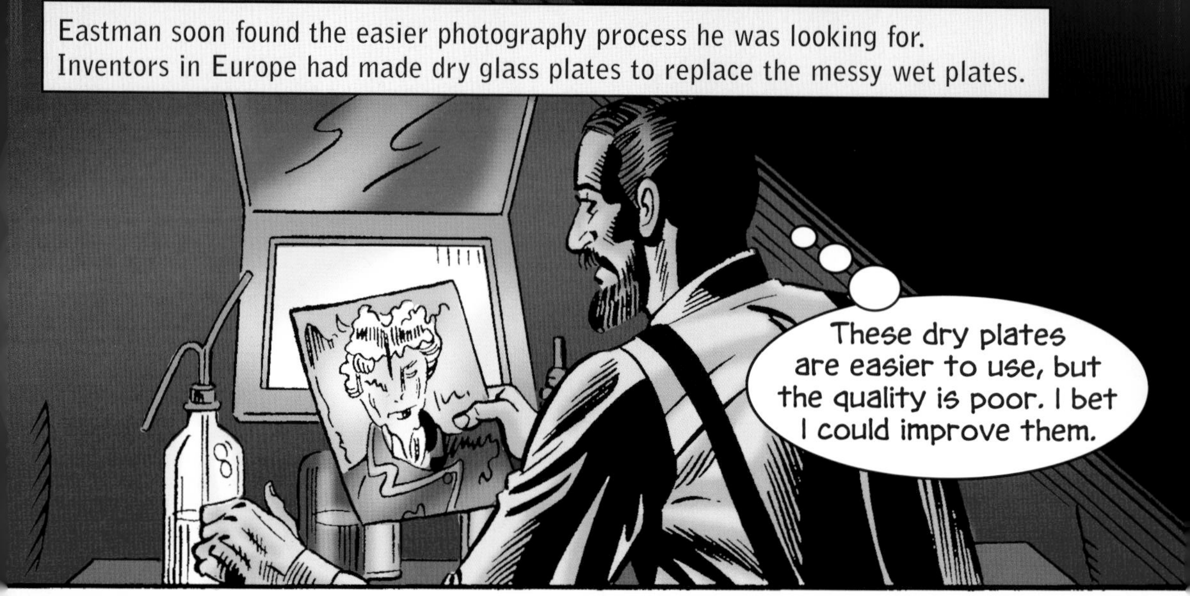
Eastman soon found the easier photography process he was looking for. Inventors in Europe had made dry glass plates to replace the messy wet plates.
These dry plates are easier to use, but the quality is poor. I bet I could improve them.

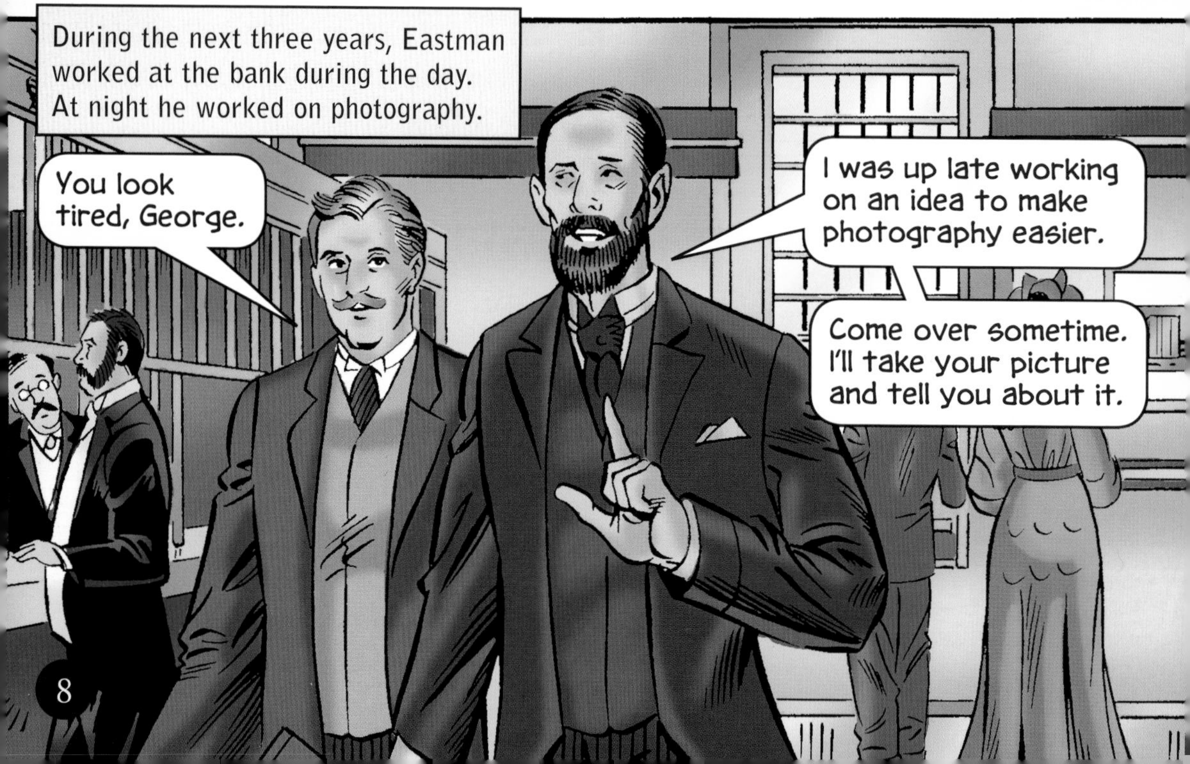
During the next three years, Eastman worked at the bank during the day. At night he worked on photography.
You look tired, George.
I was up late working on an idea to make photography easier.
Come over sometime. I'll take your picture and tell you about it.

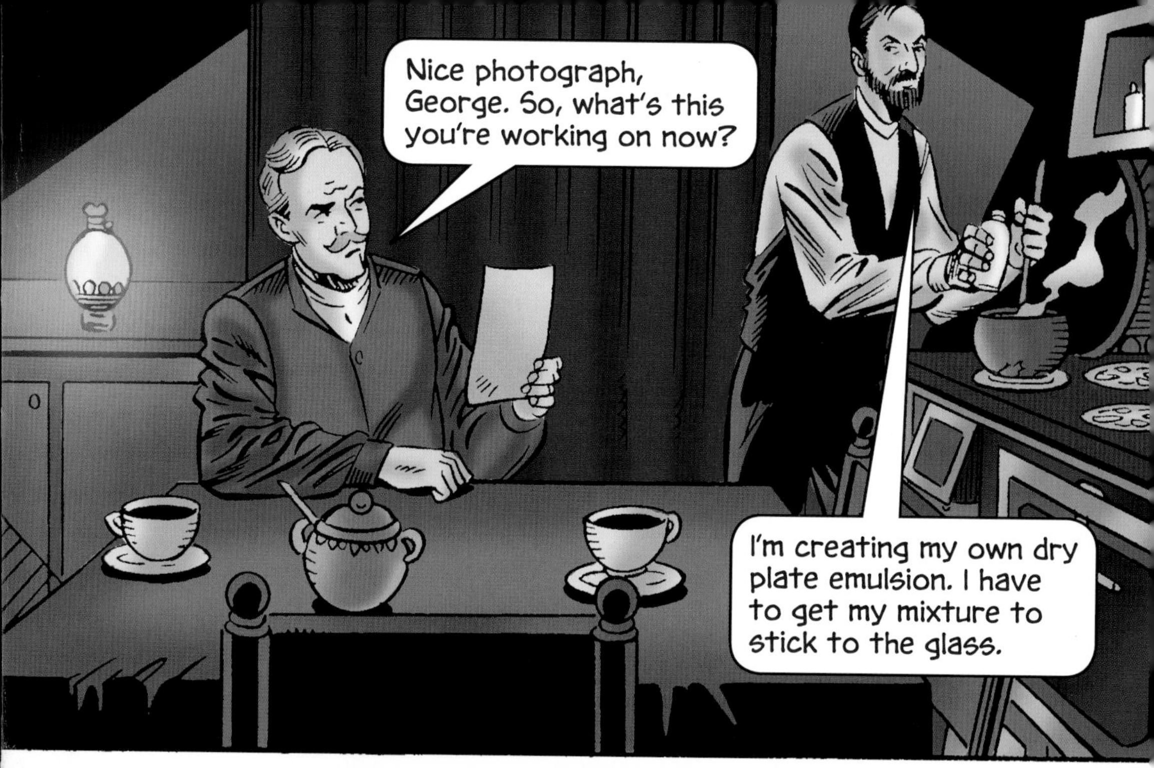
Nice photograph, George. So, what's this you're working on now?
I'm creating my own dry plate emulsion. I have to get my mixture to stick to the glass.

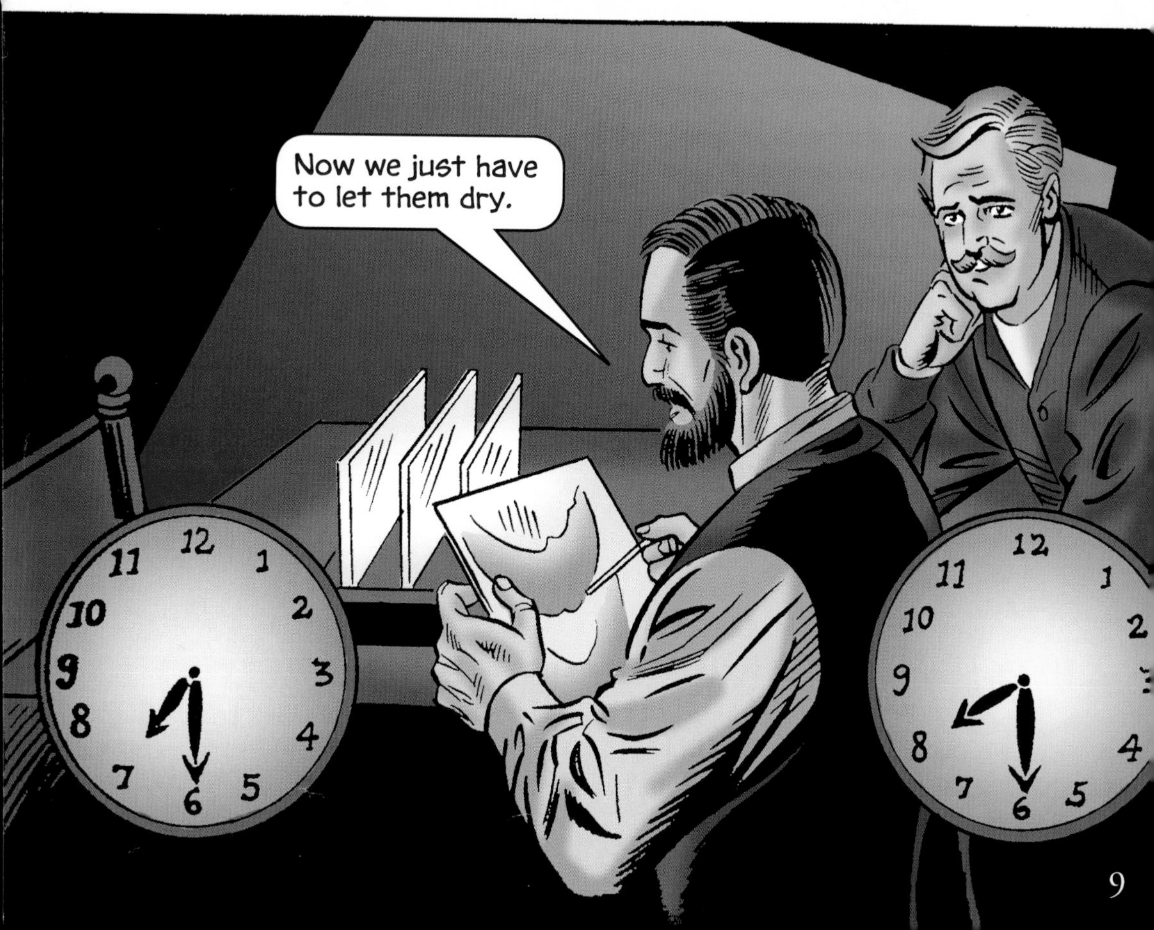
Now we just have to let them dry.

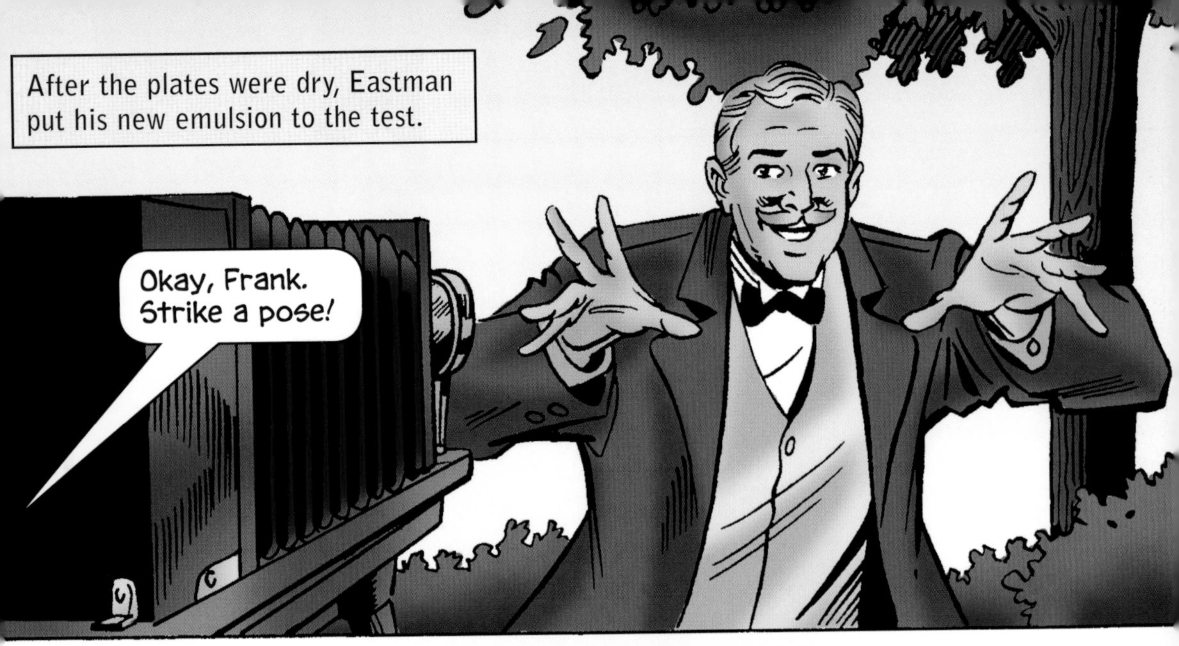
After the plates were dry, Eastman put his new emulsion to the test.
Okay, Frank. Strike a pose!

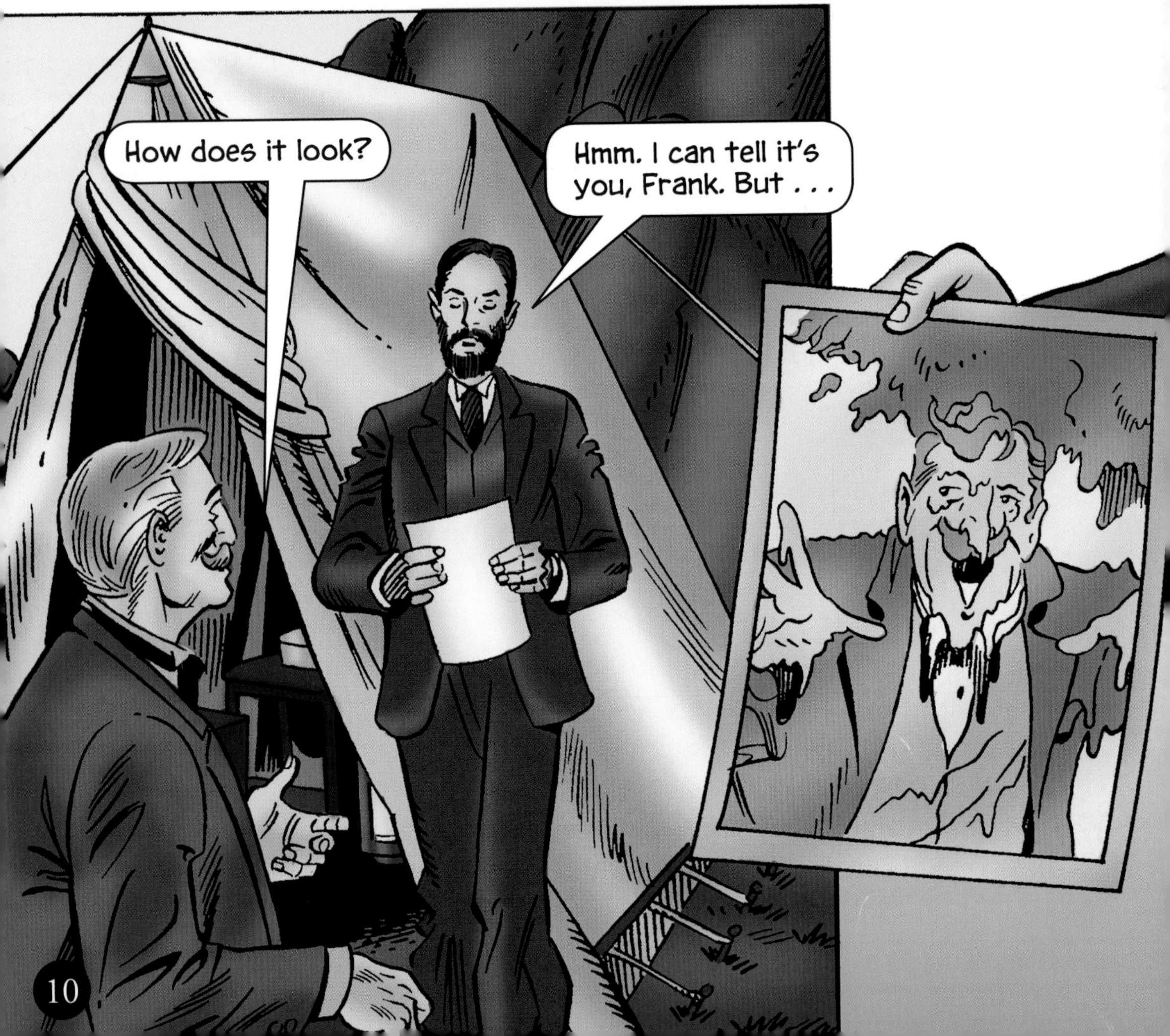
How does it look?
Hmm. I can tell it's you, Frank. But . . .

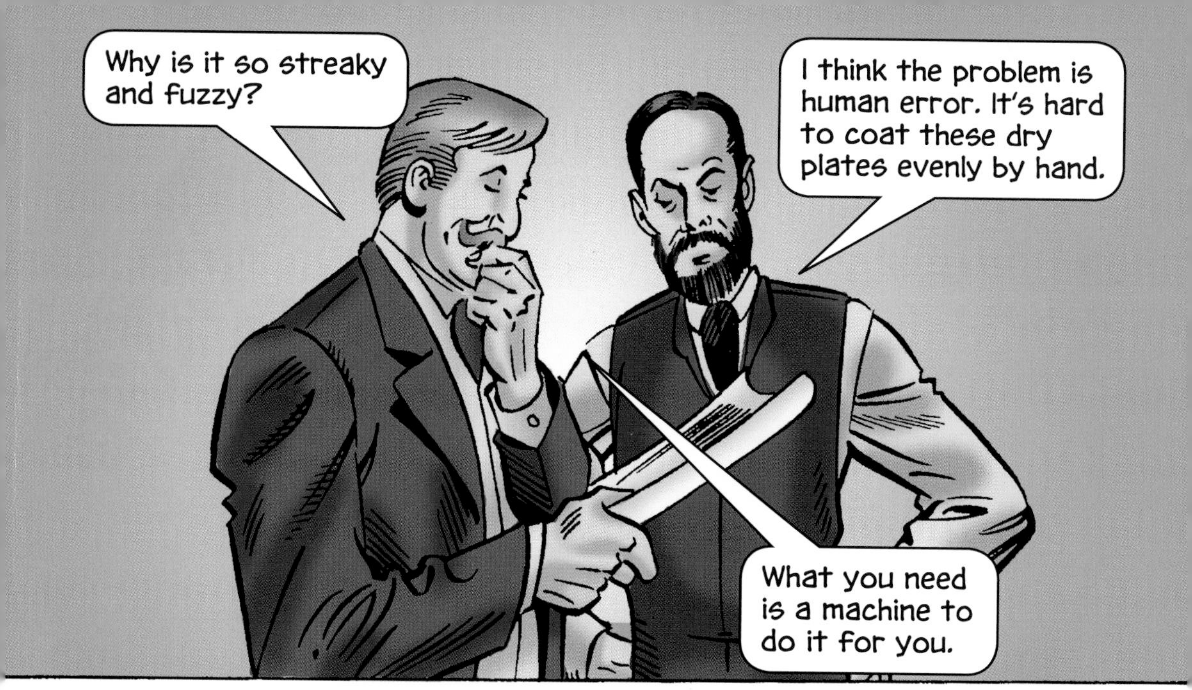
Why is it so streaky and fuzzy?
I think the problem is human error. It's hard to coat these dry plates evenly by hand.
What you need is a machine to do it for you.

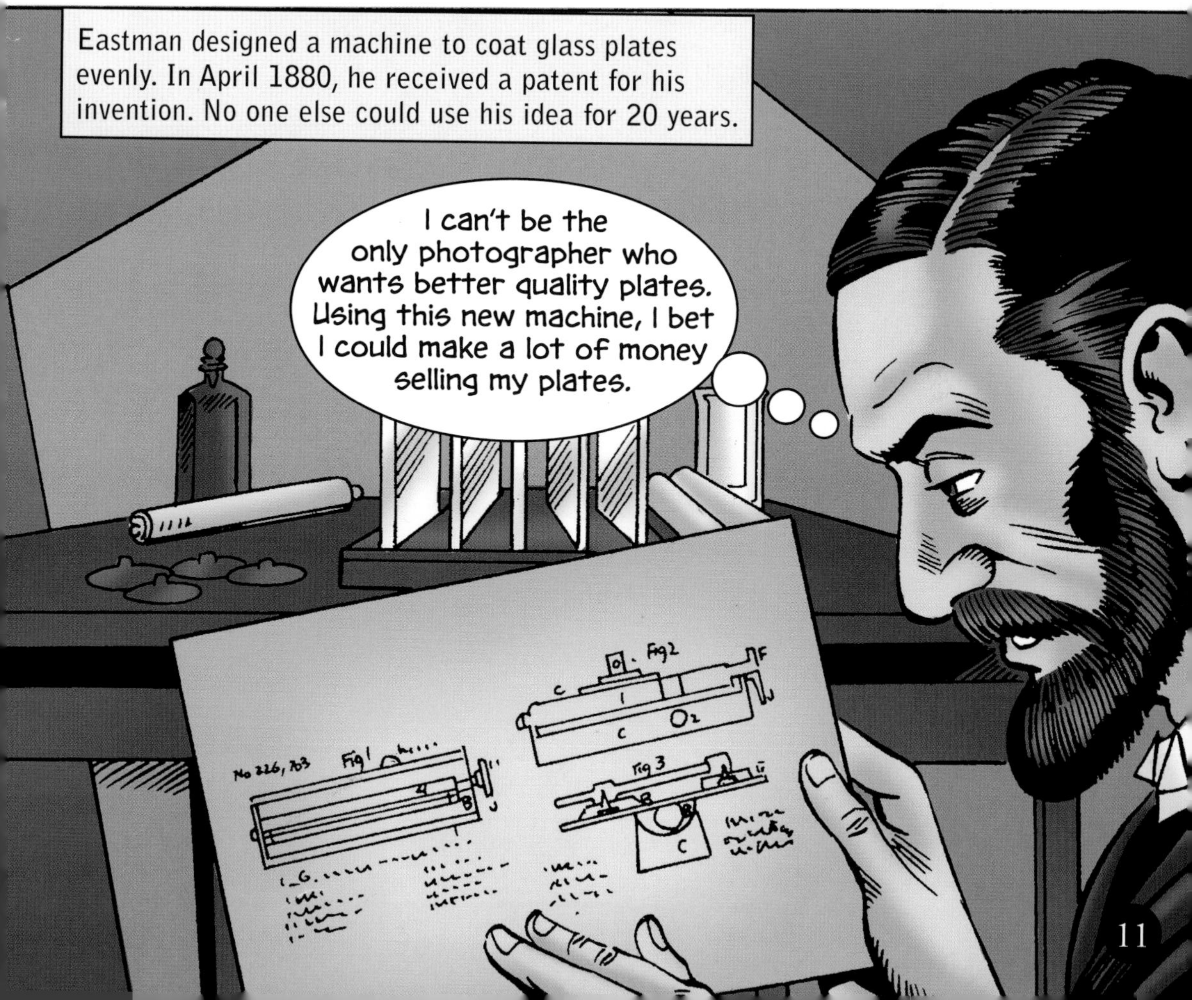
Eastman designed a machine to coat glass plates evenly. In April 1880, he received a patent for his invention. No one else could use his idea for 20 years.
I can't be the only photographer who wants better quality plates. Using this new machine, I bet I could make a lot of money selling my plates.

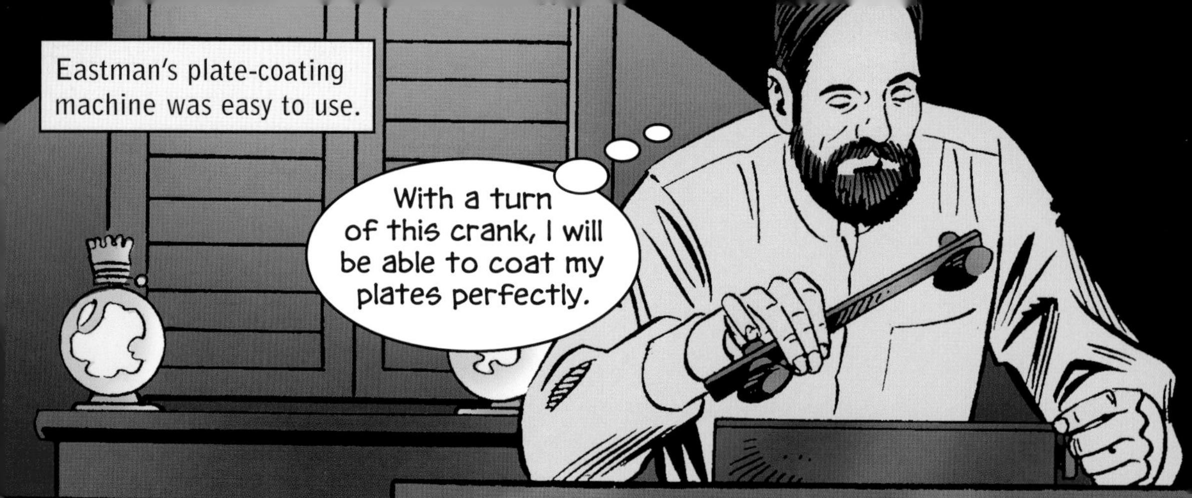
Eastman's plate-coating machine was easy to use.
With a turn of this crank, I will be able to coat my plates perfectly.

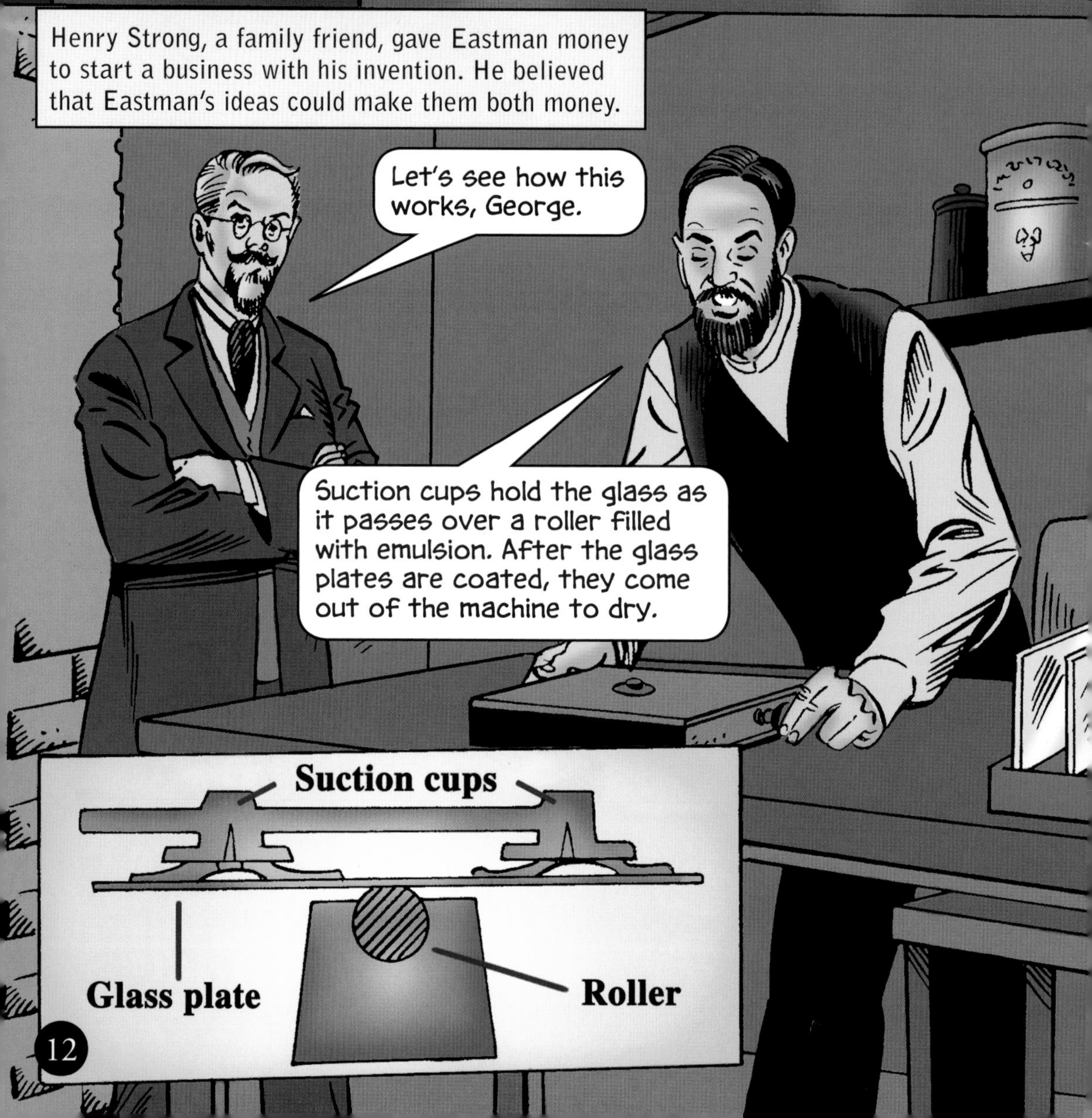
Henry Strong, a family friend, gave Eastman money to start a business with his invention. He believed that Eastman's ideas could make them both money.
Let's see how this works, George.
Suction cups hold the glass as it passes over a roller filled with emulsion. After the glass plates are coated, they come out of the machine to dry.
Suction cups
Glass plate
Roller

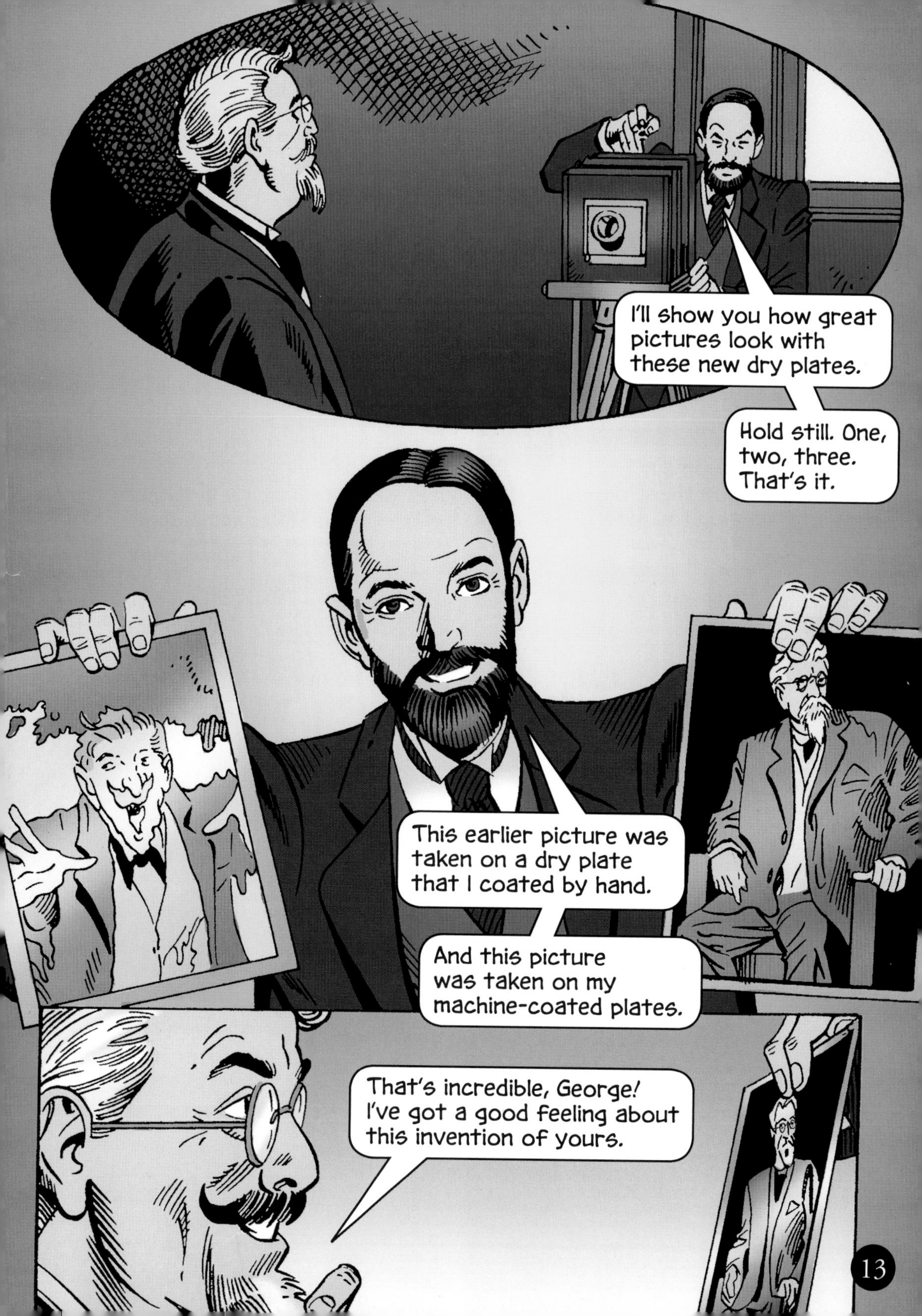
I'll show you how great pictures look with these new dry plates.
Hold still. One, two, three. That's it.
This earlier picture was taken on a dry plate that I coated by hand.
And this picture was taken on my machine-coated plates.
That's incredible, George! I've got a good feeling about this invention of yours.

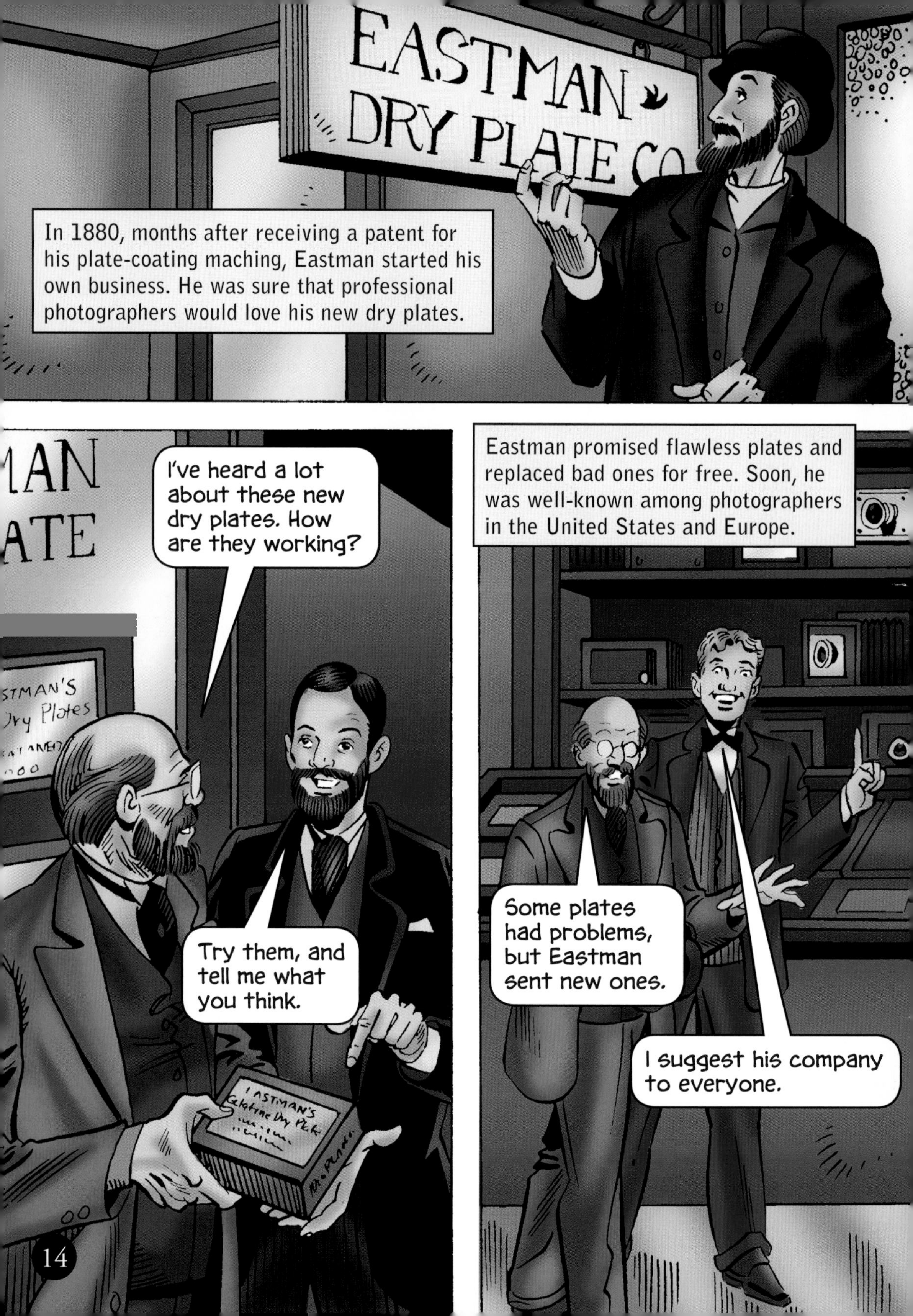
EASTMAN
DRY PLATE CO
In 1880, months after receiving a patent for his plate-coating maching, Eastman started his own business. He was sure that professional photographers would love his new dry plates.
I've heard a lot about these new dry plates. How are they working?
Try them, and tell me what you think.
Eastman promised flawless plates and replaced bad ones for free. Soon, he was well-known among photographers in the United States and Europe.
Some plates had problems, but Eastman sent new ones.
I suggest his company to everyone.

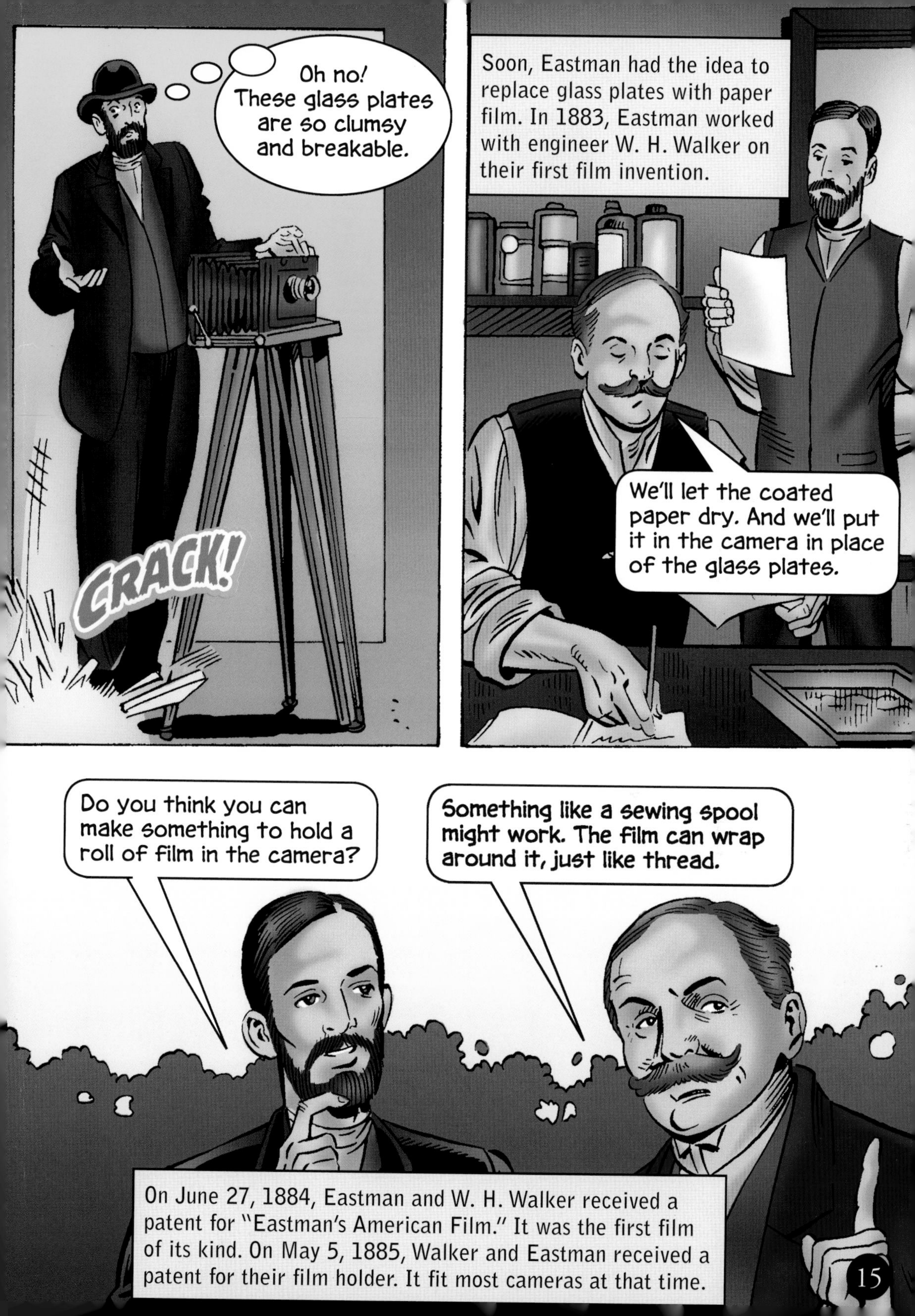
Oh no! These glass plates are so clumsy and breakable.
CRACK!
Soon, Eastman had the idea to replace glass plates with paper film. In 1883, Eastman worked with engineer W. H. Walker on their first film invention.
We'll let the coated paper dry. And we'll put it in the camera in place of the glass plates.
Do you think you can make something to hold a roll of film in the camera?
Something like a sewing spool might work. The film can wrap around it, just like thread.
On June 27, 1884, Eastman and W. H. Walker received a patent for "Eastman's American Film." It was the first film of its kind. On May 5, 1885, Walker and Eastman received a patent for their film holder. It fit most cameras at that time.

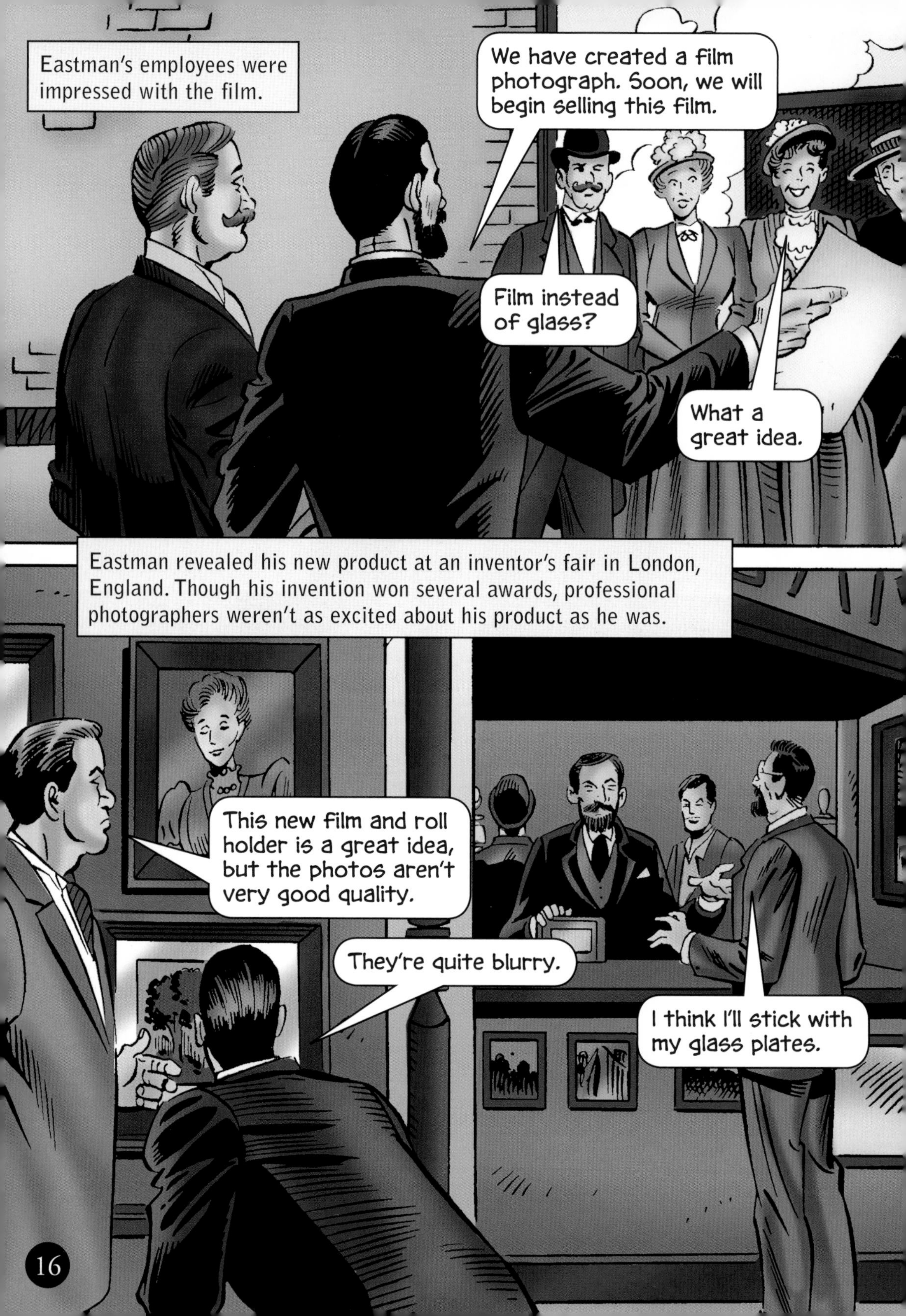
Eastman's employees were impressed with the film.
We have created a film photograph. Soon, we will begin selling this film.
Film instead of glass?
What a great idea.
Eastman revealed his new product at an inventor's fair in London, England. Though his invention won several awards, professional photographers weren't as excited about his product as he was.
This new film and roll holder is a great idea, but the photos aren't very good quality.
They're quite blurry.
I think I'll stick with my glass plates.

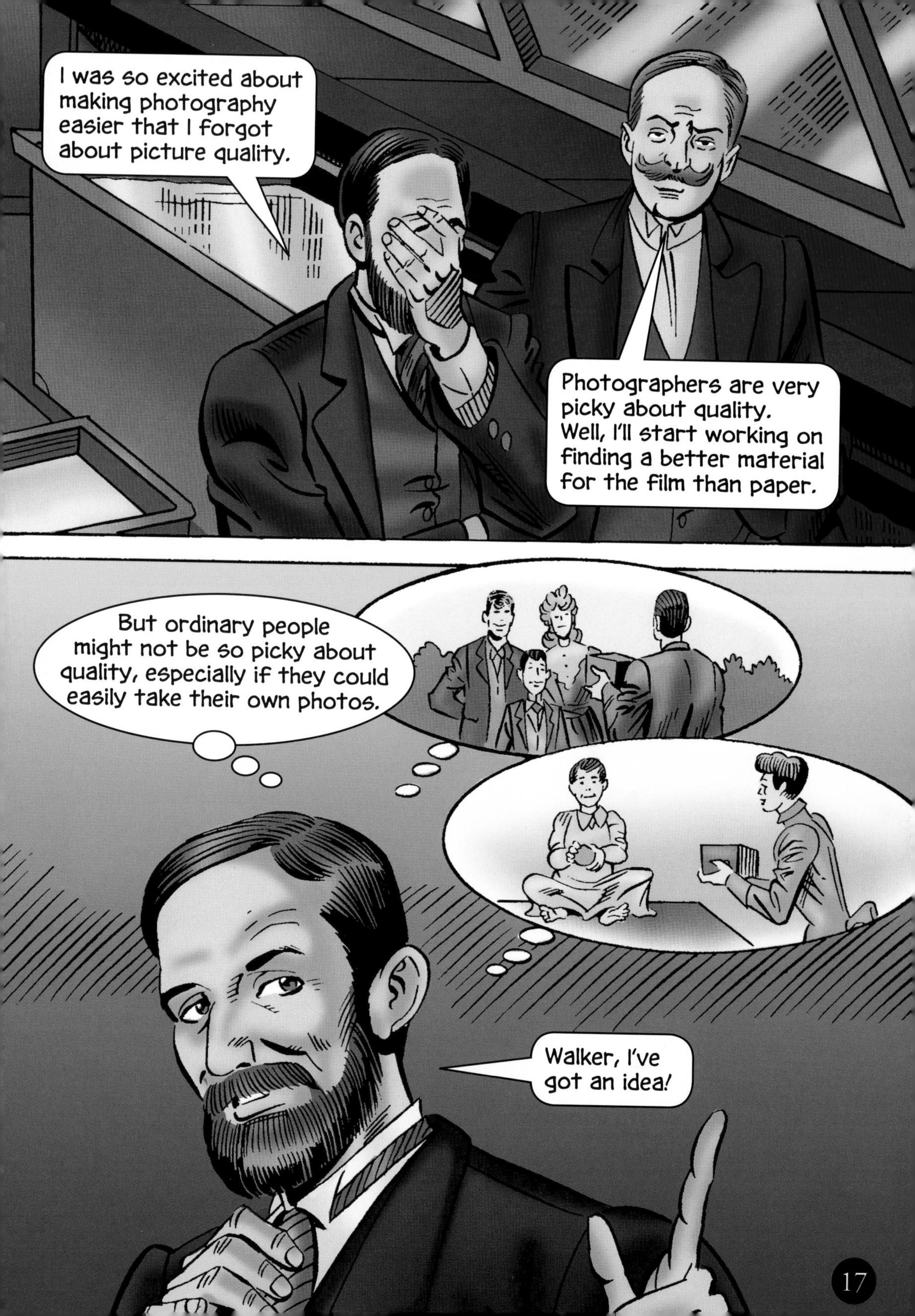
I was so excited about making photography easier that I forgot about picture quality.
Photographers are very picky about quality. Well, I'll start working on finding a better material for the film than paper.
But ordinary people might not be so picky about quality, especially if they could easily take their own photos.
Walker, I've got an idea!

CHAPTER 3

BRINGING PHOTOGRAPHY TO THE PEOPLE

While Walker worked on making a better film, Eastman created a new type of camera. He had a cabinetmaker build the camera casing. A local machinist made a shutter that took photos quicker than other cameras. And an optical shop, owned by German immigrants named Bausch and Lomb, supplied Eastman with a camera lens.

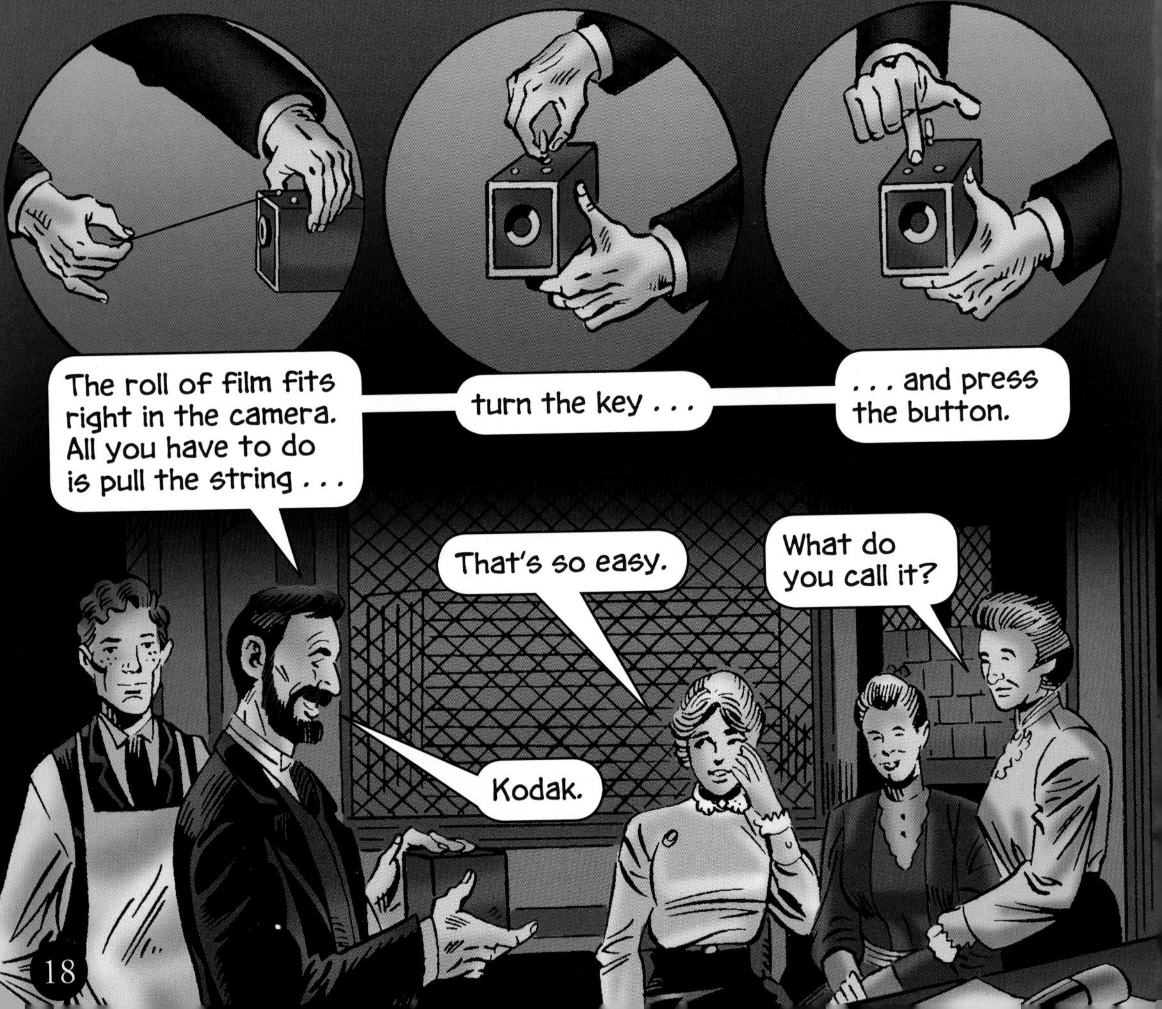

The roll of film fits right in the camera. All you have to do is pull the string . . .
turn the key . . .
. . . and press the button.
That's so easy.
What do you call it?
Kodak.

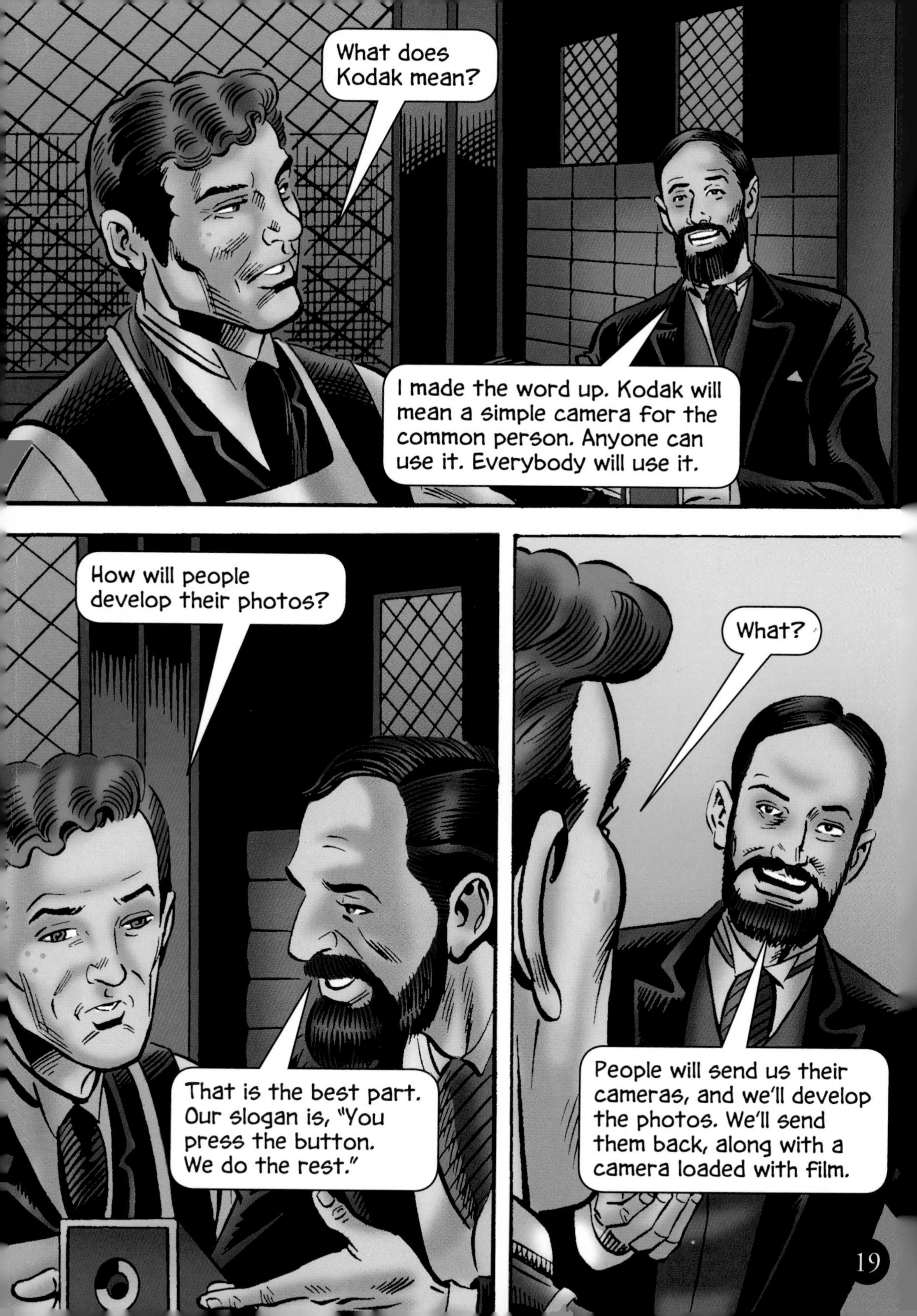
What does Kodak mean?
I made the word up. Kodak will mean a simple camera for the common person. Anyone can use it. Everybody will use it.
How will people develop their photos?
That is the best part. Our slogan is, "You press the button. We do the rest."
What?
People will send us their cameras, and we'll develop the photos. We'll send them back, along with a camera loaded with film.

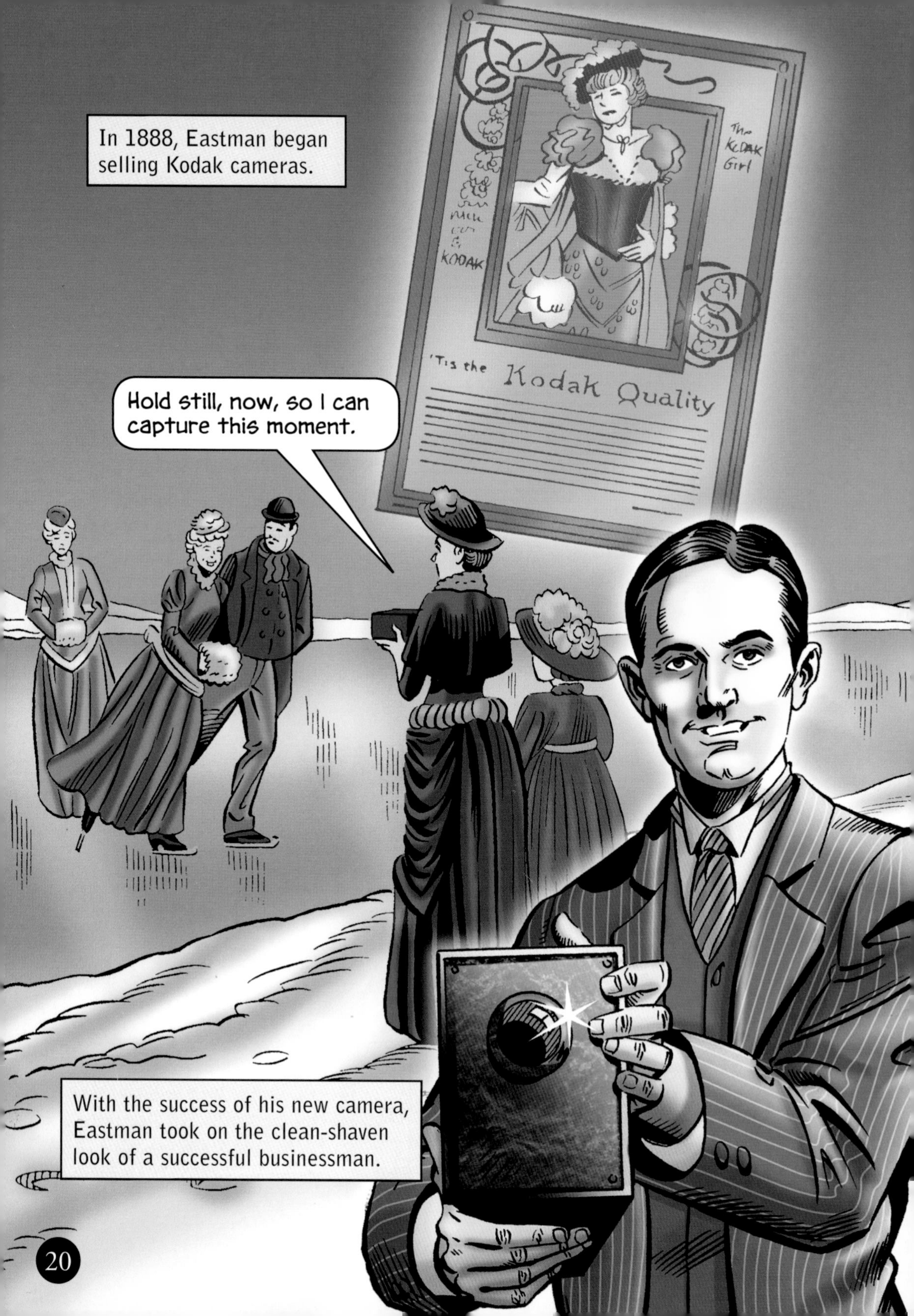

In 1888, Eastman began selling Kodak cameras.
The KODAK Girl
KODAK
'Tis the Kodak Quality
Hold still, now, so I can capture this moment.
With the success of his new camera, Eastman took on the clean-shaven look of a successful businessman.

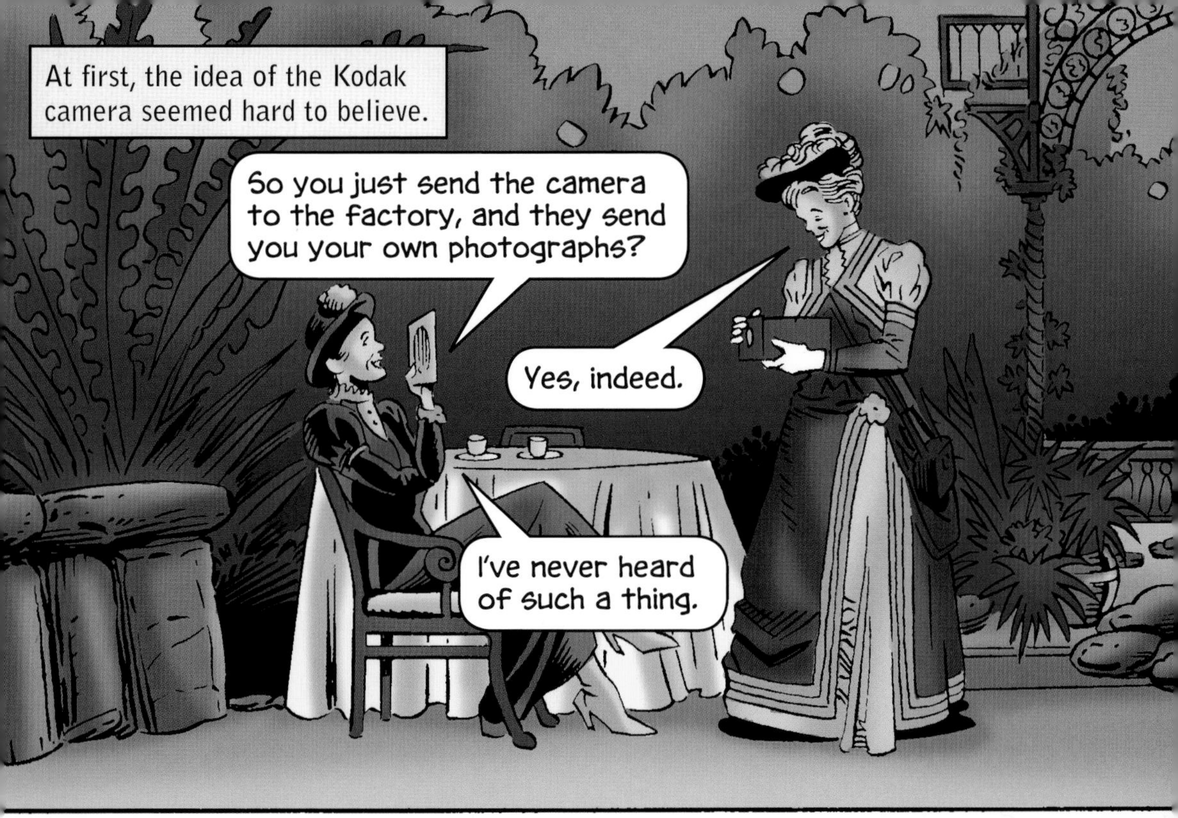
At first, the idea of the Kodak camera seemed hard to believe.
So you just send the camera to the factory, and they send you your own photographs?
Yes, indeed.
I've never heard of such a thing.

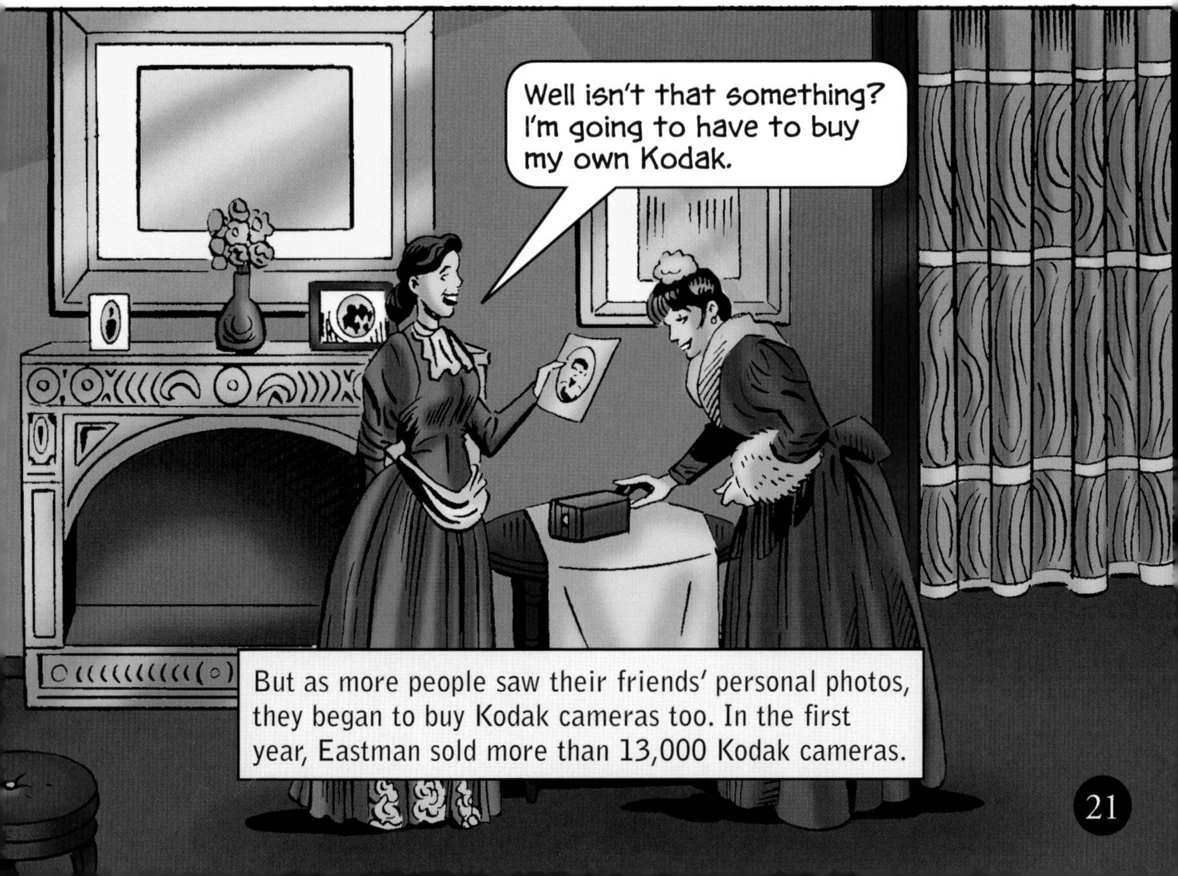
Well isn't that something? I'm going to have to buy my own Kodak.
But as more people saw their friends' personal photos, they began to buy Kodak cameras too. In the first year, Eastman sold more than 13,000 Kodak cameras.

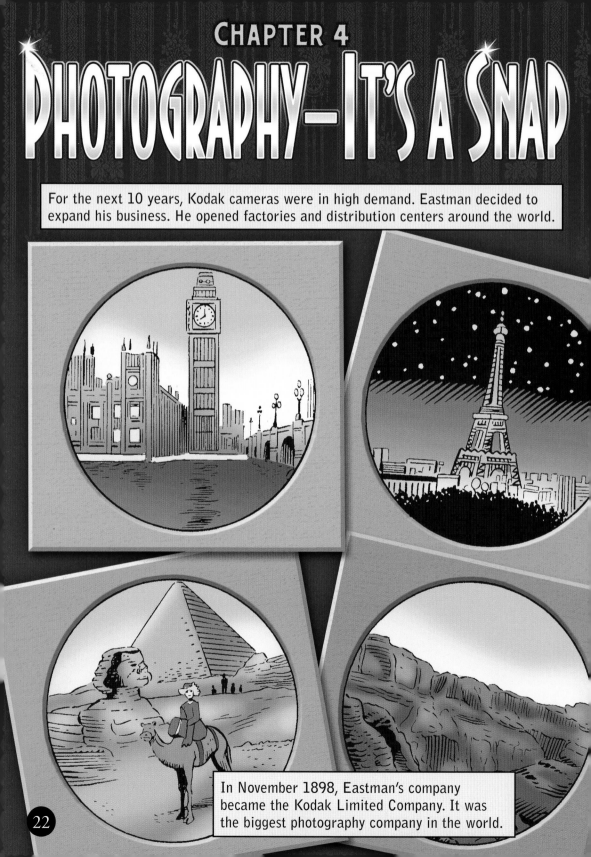

CHAPTER 4
PHOTOGRAPHY—IT'S A SNAP

For the next 10 years, Kodak cameras were in high demand. Eastman decided to expand his business. He opened factories and distribution centers around the world.

In November 1898, Eastman's company became the Kodak Limited Company. It was the biggest photography company in the world.

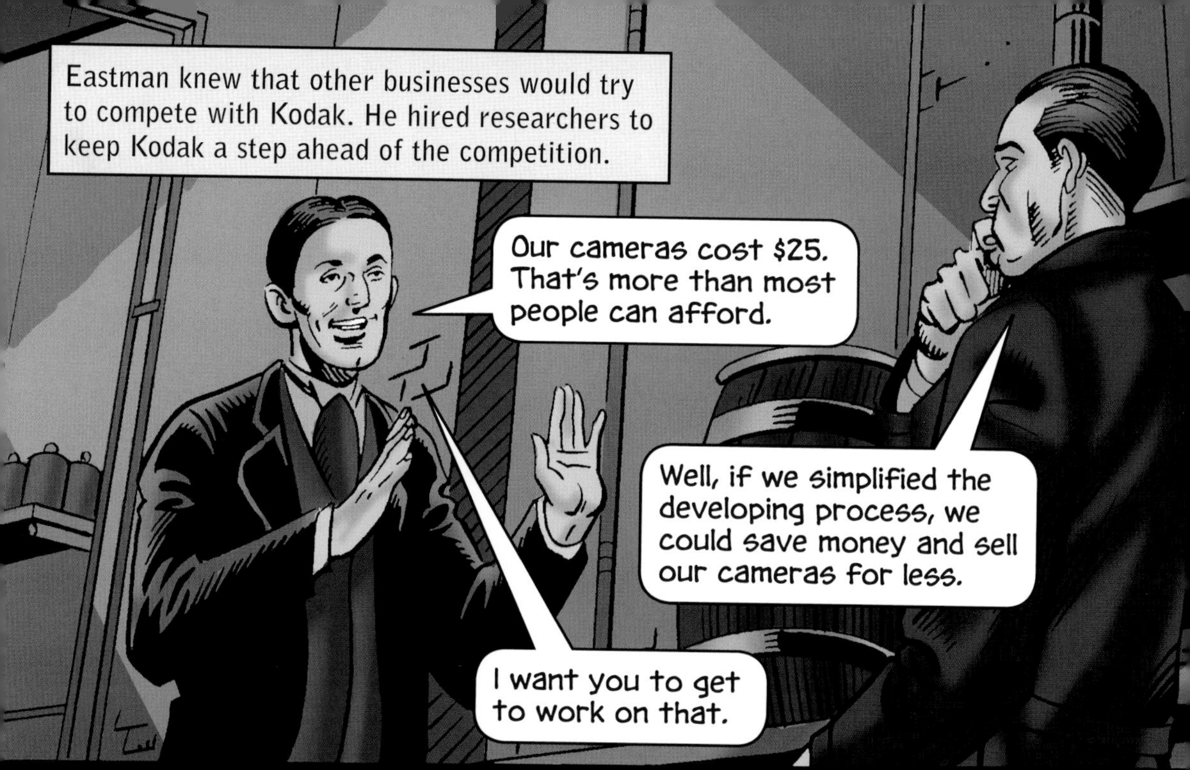
Eastman knew that other businesses would try to compete with Kodak. He hired researchers to keep Kodak a step ahead of the competition.
Our cameras cost $25. That's more than most people can afford.
Well, if we simplified the developing process, we could save money and sell our cameras for less.
I want you to get to work on that.

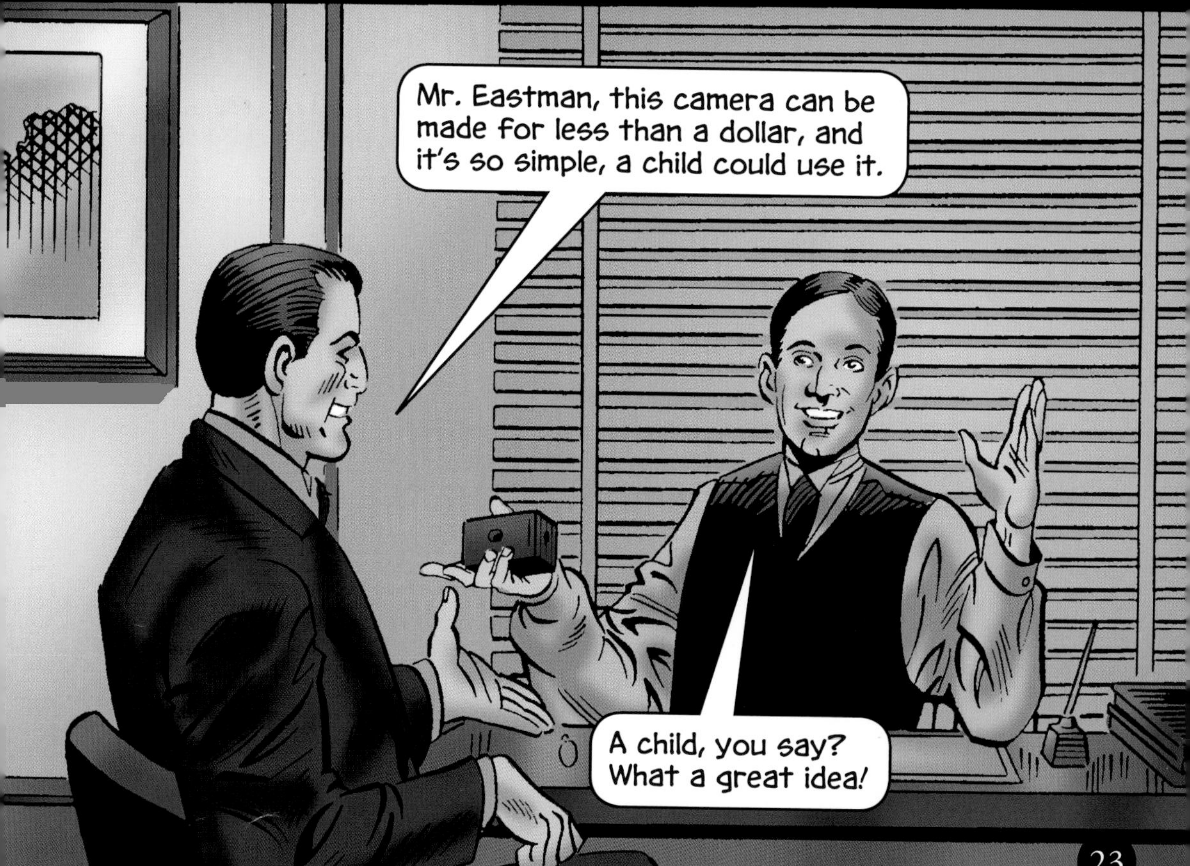
Mr. Eastman, this camera can be made for less than a dollar, and it's so simple, a child could use it.
A child, you say? What a great idea!

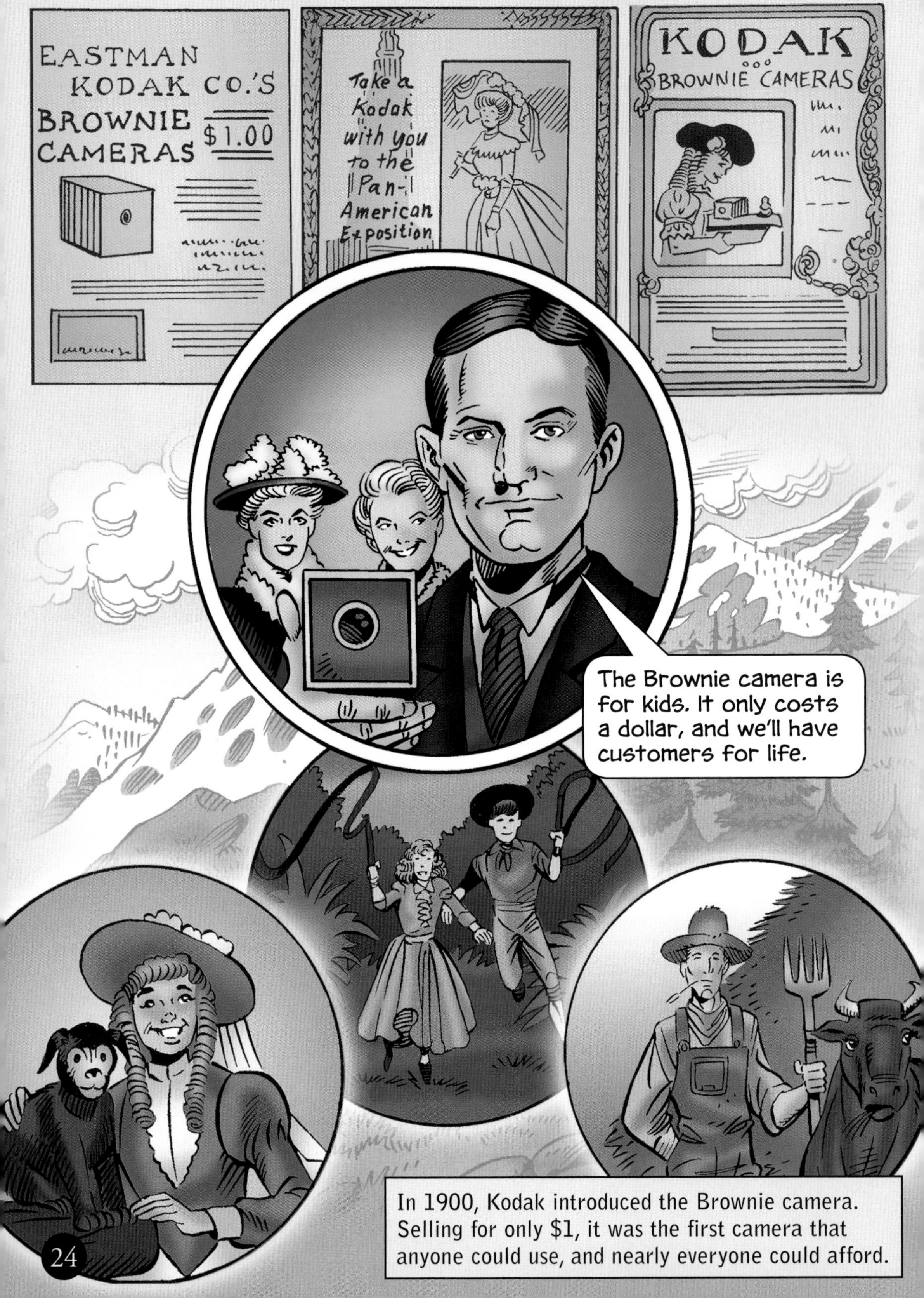
EASTMAN KODAK CO.'S BROWNIE CAMERAS $1.00
Take a Kodak with you to the Pan-American Exposition
KODAK BROWNIE CAMERAS
The Brownie camera is for kids. It only costs a dollar, and we'll have customers for life.
In 1900, Kodak introduced the Brownie camera. Selling for only $1, it was the first camera that anyone could use, and nearly everyone could afford.

True to form, Eastman continued to improve the Brownie. The popular camera eventually went through 25 changes, including adding color and flash photography.
BROWNIE CAMERA
Wow! My own Brownie camera. Thanks, Uncle Dan.
I remember how much fun I had taking pictures with my first Brownie.

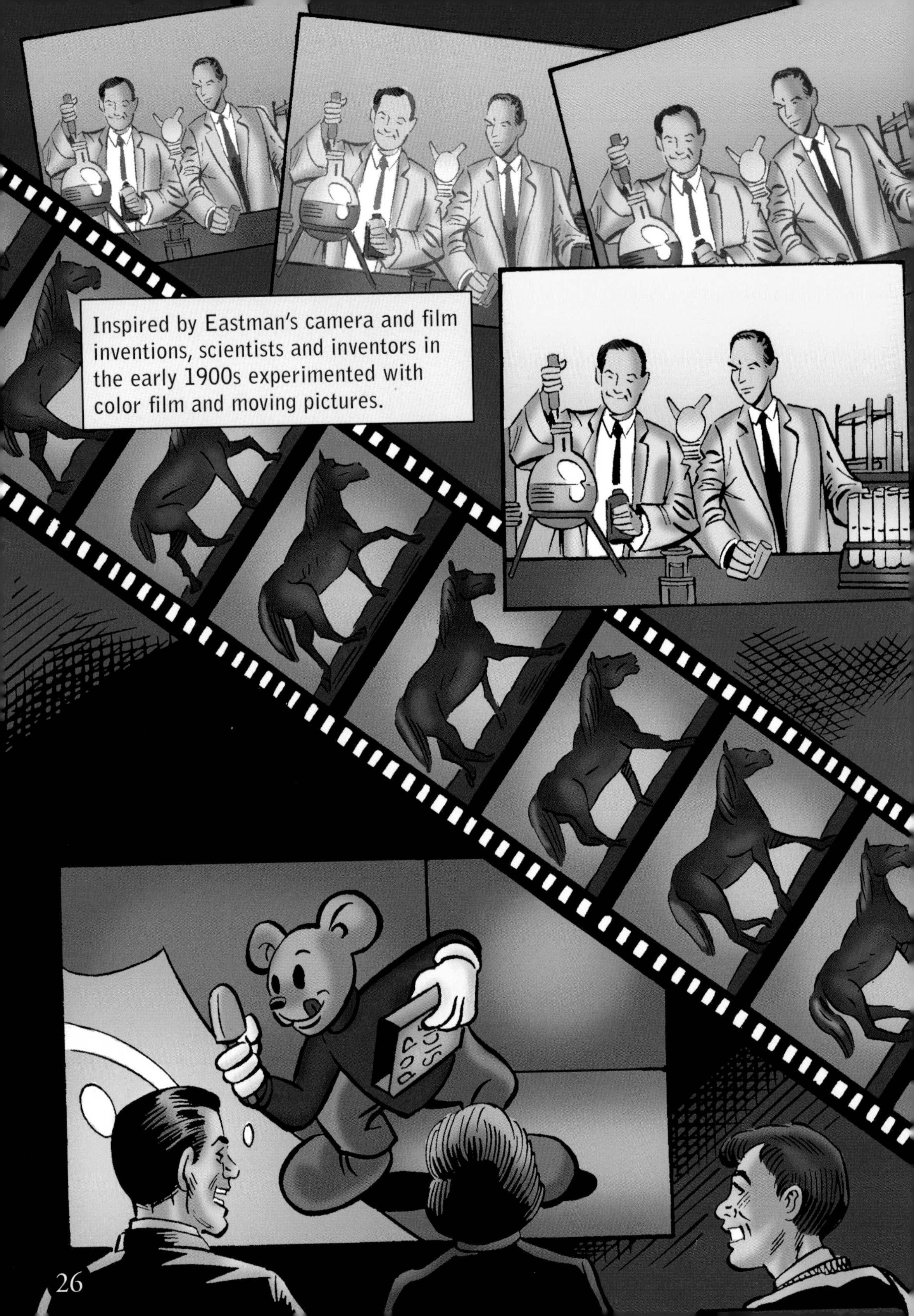
Inspired by Eastman's camera and film inventions, scientists and inventors in the early 1900s experimented with color film and moving pictures.
POP SICLE

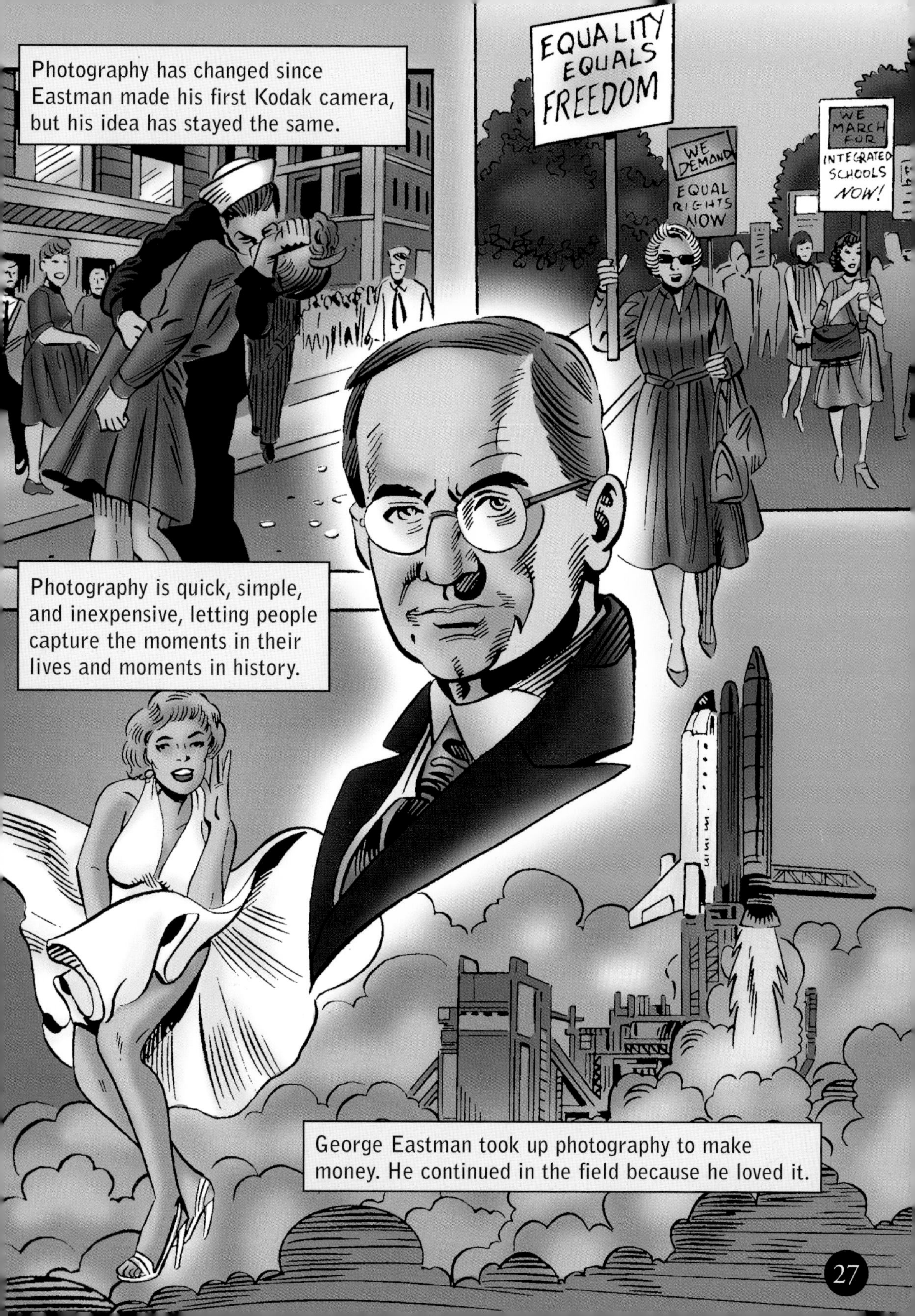
Photography has changed since Eastman made his first Kodak camera, but his idea has stayed the same.
EQUALITY EQUALS FREEDOM
WE DEMAND EQUAL RIGHTS NOW
WE MARCH FOR INTEGRATED SCHOOLS NOW!
Photography is quick, simple, and inexpensive, letting people capture the moments in their lives and moments in history.
George Eastman took up photography to make money. He continued in the field because he loved it.

MORE ABOUT
GEORGE EASTMAN
AND KODAK

 George Eastman was born July 12, 1854 in a small town outside of Rochester, New York. He died March 14, 1932.

 Eastman didn't finish high school. When his father died, Eastman quit school at age 14 to help support the family. He worked as an office messenger boy.

 Eastman's first Kodak camera was sold for $25. This included a roll of film for taking 100 pictures. Customers sent their cameras to the company once they took all their pictures. They paid $10 to have their film developed and their camera shipped back to them with a new roll of film.

 Eastman became a millionaire, but he gave much of his money away to universities, schools in poor communities, and the arts.

 In 1826, Frenchman Joseph Nicephore Niepce made the first surviving photograph.

In the 1800s, many people tried to improve photography before Eastman. Inventors used different chemicals on all types of materials, such as glass, tin, and paper.

 The word photograph comes from two Greek words. The word *photo* means "light," and *graph* means to "write or draw." To photograph then means to write or draw with light. In the early years of photography, people captured images with sunlight and a combination of chemicals.

 Thomas Edison, the inventor of the lightbulb, helped develop the motion picture camera for showing movies.

Eastman introduced Kodacolor color film in 1928.

GLOSSARY

develop (duh-VEL-up)—using chemicals to change film into photographs

emulsion (ee-MUHL-shun)—chemical coating in a thin gelatin layer on photographic film, paper, or glass

expose (ek-SPOZE)—to let light fall onto photographic plates or film

film (FILM)—a lightweight plastic that you put in a camera to take pictures

shutter (SHUHT-ur)—the part of a camera that opens to expose film to light when a picture is taken

INTERNET SITES

FactHound offers a safe, fun way to find Internet sites related to this book. All of the sites on FactHound have been researched by our staff.

Here's how:
1. Visit *www.facthound.com*
2. Choose your grade level.
3. Type in this book ID **0736868488** for age-appropriate sites. You may also browse subjects by clicking on letters, or by clicking on pictures and words.
4. Click on the **Fetch It** button.

FactHound will fetch the best sites for you!

READ MORE

Aller, Susan Bivin. *George Eastman.* History Maker Bios. Minneapolis: Lerner, 2004.

Bridgman, Roger. *1,000 Inventions and Discoveries.* London: Dorling Kindersley Limited, 2002.

Graham, Ian. *Film and Photography.* Communications Close-Up. Austin, Texas: Raintree Steck-Vaughn, 2001.

Johnson, Neil. *National Geographic Photography Guide for Kids.* Washington, D.C.: National Geographic Society, 2001.

Pflueger, Lynda. *George Eastman: Bringing Photography to the People.* Historical American Biographies. Berkeley Heights, N.J.: Enslow, 2002.

BIBLIOGRAPHY

Brayer, Elizabeth. *George Eastman: A Biography.* Baltimore: Johns Hopkins University Press, 1996.

Collins, Douglas. *The Story of Kodak.* New York: Harry N. Abrams, 1990.

Davenport, Alma. *The History of Photography: An Overview.* Boston: Focal Press, 1991.

Kodak Corporate Home Page. *The History of Kodak.* http://www.kodak.com/US/en/corp/kodakHistory/index.shtml.

INDEX